As Time Goes By
The Occupation Years

Introduction

This book offers a unique collection of fascinating images of the German Occupation
of Jersey from 1940 - 1945, many of which have never been published before.
They are shown here alongside a recent up-to-date comparison
of the same location to show just how much the Island has or,
in some cases, has not changed with the passing years.
We hope you will enjoy this glimpse back into the Occupation years
and will take note of our ever changing Island "As Time Goes By"

One month before the outbreak of World War Two. This is the Battle of Flowers in August 1939 and the float "Peace to all Nations" which was inspired by Chamberlain's famous speech in 1938 after his meeting with Adolf Hitler.

Note "Chamberlain" and "Hitler" with other characters on and around the float.

The 2005 Battle of Flowers and the Parish of Grouville float called 'Ganesh' which means Indian Festival of Fortune. It won the Grand Prix des Paroisse (Best Parish) trophy as well as the best costume and best moonlight carnival atmosphere trophies.

This bunker was a 625/626 casement for a 7.5 cm anti-tank gun and was built in early 1944. It was painted to look like a bungalow and the gun fired its first test shot on 6th June 1944.

The majority of bunkers remain in the Island today as they were too difficult and expensive to remove. The one in the left-hand picture, however, was an exception and was demolished in 1973

The officer in the centre is Major-General Graf von Schmettow outside the Don Hotel in The Parade.

The Don is a Randalls pub that is still popular today.

Two children watch troops march past outside the Bagot Inn in 1942

Randalls still own the Bagot Inn but they no longer brew their own beer.

Senior N.C.Os of Machine Gun Battalion 16 relax outside the Carrefour Selous pub in St Lawrence.

Carrefour Selous closed as a pub in the1990s after many years of trading. It is now Club Carrefour Health & Beauty.
Here Peter Booth and Sally Leftwich take in the sunshine in the same spot.

This soldier later lost his dog and placed an advert in the JEP in 1944 to find it. He was eventually reunited with the dog.

This is now a very busy junction with six lanes of traffic. The addition of the modern buildings at Fort Regent has changed the skyline.

One of the numerous parades held in The Parade. This one was in 1943. Note the white summer uniforms. In the background is the Don Monument.

This picture today shows an assortment of modern street furniture including bike parks, a bollard and a yellow telephone box. The Don Monument was built in 1885 to commemorate Lieutenant-General Sir George Don who was Lieutenant-Governor in the Island from 1806 until 1814.

Charing Cross, August 8th 1940. Note the HECT of Hectors fish and chip shop in between two of the German army soldiers.

Hector Graham opened "Hectors" fish and chip shop in 1928. There is now an open space over the road after the buildings shown in the left hand picture were pulled down. "Hectors" is still popular after all these years and is today owned and run by Paul Spears.

The style of headgear puts this Occupation photo as after mid-1943

The Town Hall remains much the same today

Victorious German troops march along La Motte Street led by a "British Bobby"

Here this lady marches home with her shopping!

At Soldatenheim II, St Brelade's Bay Hotel. (A place where the soldiers could relax and socialise)

The beach is busier now in the absence of our German 'visitors'

German Army troops at the junction of King Street and Halkett Place in 1941. Amyson Corner.

The basic lines of Halkett Place remain the same with the Central Market on the right and the elegant building of the St Helier Methodist Centre straight ahead at the end of the road.

The funeral cortège for two Frenchmen proceeding along Snow Hill. Georges Felix Dexant (46) and his son, Georges Eugene (17), were both French voluntary workers employed by the National Socialist Vehicle Corps, which did most of the transport work for the Organisation Todt. They were accidentally gassed in their lodgings at 3 Bel Royal Villas, St Lawrence on 8th July 1942. They went to bed the previous evening leaving the gas fire alight, forgetting that the gas would be cut off at 11.00pm. When the gas came on again at 6.00am they were still asleep and thus overcome. Over 100 mourners followed the two hearses to the Strangers' Cemetery at Westmount.

In contrast this is Snow Hill, with Lower Colomberie in the background, in happier times on a sunny day.

The funeral of R.A.F. Sergeants Dennis Butlin and Abraham Holden at Westmount Cemetery on 6th June 1943. They were moved at a later date to a new Allied servicemen cemetery in Howard Davis Park. The officer is Oberleutnant Zepernick who was himself killed, shortly after this, when an R.A.F. fighter attacked the train on which he was travelling home on leave at Vire, Normandy. His body was brought back to Jersey and buried at St Brelade's Military Cemetery in November 1943.

Westmount Cemetery today. The pillars and the small building remain in place.

German Army troops march down La Route du Petit Port, St Brelade in 1941.
Note the road widening in progress. This was part of a job creation scheme set up by the States Department of Labour to avoid men having to work for the Germans in order to survive.

There are far more trees and bushes on this hill now than in 1941, so the sea is almost completely out of view. What you can see though, at the bottom of the road, is evidence of building work after the demolition of the Sea Crest Hotel and Restaurant to make way for flats.

Stabsfeldwebel Alfred Knipps from Artillery Regiment 319 at Georgetown Park Estate in 1942. Seen here sitting on a requisitioned 1939 MG Sports Saloon, he was last heard of pig farming in Lincolnshire.

The registration number J11347 is now on a grey Ferguson tractor seen here with Raoul Le Mière on the family farm in St Lawrence. The background of Georgetown Park Estate remains fairly similar.

The Luftwaffe band entering The Parade for the grand "Victory Parade" on 8th August 1940.
Note the German Swastika flag flying from the Town Hall.

Here some original buildings remain in place while others have been re-built.

Charing Cross in July 1941. Again another Randalls Beers advert and of course Jersey ice cream.
Mr Louis is the ice cream seller. Note the German propaganda vehicle over the road on the left of the picture.

There are lots of things different in this picture. Sand Street car park and the new Thomas Cook building are relatively new additions. Note also some new artwork - Gordon Young's 'Crapaud Sculpture' and Nicholas Romeril's 'Herd of Charing Cross.'

Three German officers taking in the view at St Brelade's Bay in 1943. Note civilians were still allowed on the beach at this time.

There are many more people using the beach now. Note also all the new buildings around the bay.

Part of the crowd, next to the Cenotaph, listening to the band in 1940.

Lloyds Pharmacy now replaces A.H. Copp, the tobacco merchants. The area around the Cenotaph is still a pleasant open space where people can relax.

1941 and an early type look-out post at Corbière.

Nowadays locals and tourists alike enjoy the views around Corbière.

A Morris 8 Open Tourer at the end of the Albert Pier long before the dome etc. were added to Fort Regent.

Car courtesy of Motor Mall

The background here has changed dramatically with not much else other than the original parts of Fort Regent and the back of the La Folie Inn (Just above the car bonnet) remaining the same.
The sports cars today have also changed dramatically. This is a Lotus Elise capable of a top speed of 150 mph.

Charing Cross, St Helier in July, 1941

Nearly all of these buildings remain in place today. Once again we see another example of Nicholas Romeril's 'Herd of Charing Cross' artwork over The Luggage Shop.

Looking towards the Harbour in 1941. P.C.Howe and P.C.Gray are on duty. No doubt another photo opportunity for the propaganda unit.

In 1995 this area was landscaped and re-named to mark the 50th anniversary of Liberation and is now known as Liberation Square with the Liberation Statue on the left-hand side. Note the sign on the building on the right that still houses the men's public toilets.

"Occupiers and the occupied" photo shoot in the Parade Gardens in 1940. Notice the interesting characters on the bench.

The railings shown in the picture on the left have now been removed but note the edge of the Don Monument which, if you look very carefully, is also just visible in the Occupation picture.

A company taken from Infantry Regiment 582 drawn up on the Albert Pier to form a Guard of Honour to greet Field Marshal von Witzleben on the occasion of his visit on 11th July 1941. The officer is Colonel von Schlotheim, C.O. of Infantry Regiment 582.

52

The wall and railings still remain in good condition today.

P.C. Renouf and Dr Bleckwenn, senior medical officer with Field Command 515, in the winter of 1943/44. Note the "To Weymouth Boat" sign still in place. It would be a while before the boat ran again.

The "Ask for *Mary Ann*" sign is still there today on the Southampton Hotel

German Air force and Navy personnel on the town end of the Albert Pier in August 1940.

Now a yacht marina with a lot more new building in the background, again including the dome etc of Fort Regent.

German troops marching down The Parade. They dressed like this for sports events and fitness training.

Note the addition of the General Hospital at the top end of The Parade.

On duty in the harbour area.

Once again we see the La Folie Inn in the background looking very similar to the way it looked over sixty years ago.

Insel Soldaten Choir on 5th July 1943 outside Wests Cinema in Bath Street. The Germans used the attached Plaza Ballroom for various purposes, including lectures, until late 1943.

West Centre as it looks today complete with cows.

A guided tour of Gorey Castle - inspecting the spoils of war.

Part of the wall on the right has been removed. Note the introduction of the new layer on top of the turrets which the Germans used as lookout posts.

German troops walking along St Saviour's Road.

The features of some of these buildings still remain.

Naval transport with German cars and locally requisitioned lorries in 1944 outside the Pomme d'Or Hotel which was being used as the German naval headquarters.

Note the new façade of the Pomme D'or Hotel while the Southampton Hotel remains much the same.

A crowded scene in The Parade, St Helier beside an interesting example of the public transport of the day. Somewhat different to the buses on our roads now.

Since September 2002, the Island's bus service has been operated by Connex Transport Jersey Ltd on behalf of the States of Jersey. Connex has operations in over 25 countries throughout the world. In Jersey, the Mybus network has carried over seven million passengers in its first three years of operation.

Funeral of the German Hafenkommandant (German Navy) who died of a heart attack in April 1943.

St Brelade's Church as it stands today with the very large tree in the centre still a dominant feature

May 12th 1945 and the German prisoners-of-war are marched past Commercial Buildings towards the transport boats taking them to England.

The Southampton and Royal Yacht hotels look fairly similar to the way they appeared in 1945 but the statue of Queen Victoria has moved several times since the picture on the left was taken and is now sitting in Victoria Park, opposite the Grand Hotel.

The German army marching down Cheapside on 8th August 1940. Another show of strength.

The buildings remain with some alterations. A Smart Car passes the same spot.

German troop parade in 1943 at Havre des Pas

A very similar background today.

St Catherine's made an idyllic photograph location for many German officers

German prisoners-of-war being marched down Conway Street by a British "squaddie" (seen on the right).
Note this must have been very soon after Liberation as some of the POWs have yet to remove the swastika
and eagle emblem from their jackets.

The distinctive bank buildings of Lloyds and NatWest remain unmistakable.

A military band concert in August 1940 in The Parade.

A road now cuts through here passing Cyril Le Marquand House.

German troops of Cycle Squadron 319 on exercise in St Peter's Valley in 1943.

The Vic in the Valley as it looks today after being rebuilt in the 1970s.

This picture was taken after 26th May 1942 when the Soldiers Shop (Soldatenkaufhäus) opened at Burtons. The traffic controller was Mr Le Maistre.

Burtons opened on this site in the 1930s but was taken over by the Germans during the Occupation. Many of the buildings in King Street remain the same.

Luftwaffe troops taking part in a victory parade in York Street on 8th August 1940. The tall airman on the left hand side of the group is Lt. Richard Kern, who was the first German to land in Jersey on 1st July 1940.

The road has now been narrowed and the pavements widened as part of the al fresco and traffic calming measures recently introduced.

The German army on the march in 1941. Note the house on the right was eventually demolished to make way for road widening and a block of flats.

The distinctive façade on the right-hand side of Park Stores belongs to the Mornington Hotel which was established in 1958 when the Anderson family purchased a property further down Don Road and opened it, a year or so later, as a guest house. After further acquisitions and lots of building work the Mornington Hotel was born in 1974.

The funeral of Oberleutnant Zepernick at St Brelade's Military Cemetery in November 1943.
During the First and Second World Wars this Parochial cemetery provided the resting places for the bodies of 337 German servicemen who were in the Island either as prisoners-of-war during the First World War or members of the occupying forces from 1940 to 1945.

In 1961 they were all reinterred at Mont des Huisnes, St Malo, France. On the right-hand side of the gap in the trees you can see the Golden Sands Hotel on the edge of St Brelade's Bay.

The streets echo to the sound of the jackboot again in August 1940. The Luftwaffe at the top end of The Parade. Note the cyclist on the right.

Bikes are still a popular mode of transport on the streets of St Helier.

Nicholl's Service Garage and Norman's store, seen in the background on the left hand side, are still trading from the same buildings, albeit in a different colour.

Note the Weighbridge building which handled a record amount of export potatoes to the UK in 1939 of 67,738 tons, a record never again exceeded. The building was demolished in 1970 / 1971.

The picture today, apart from Commercial Buildings, has changed considerably. Note the additions of the old Fort Regent pool, Pier Road multi-storey car park, the power station chimney and, in the foreground, part of Liberation Square.

German soldiers on a Zündapp motorbike and sidecar near the Cenotaph, St Helier.
None of the original buildings, seen here on the right-hand side of the picture, remain today, partly due to the extension of Union Street behind the Cenotaph.

The Cenotaph, built by Charles de Gruchy of grey granite from La Moye, has stood in place since 1923. Cyril Le Marquand House was only added to the landscape in 1982.

German troops look across the Harbour to Elizabeth Castle in July 1941.

A much busier harbour is shown here with the Queen Elizabeth Terminal having opened on 25th May 1989 as well as many other new constructions.

Franz Zurhorst was a teenager when he was posted to Jersey during the Occupation. From Infantry Regiment 582, 1st Batallion he is seen here in Howard Davis Park. Franz visited Jersey on holiday many times in his later life and gave us some of his photograph collection.

The statue of King George V by Sir William Reid Dick has stood near the entrance to Howard Davis Park since 1939

Hauptmann Gussek, the first Island Commandant, taking the salute from Luftwaffe troops marching up The Parade, St Helier at a victory parade on 8th August 1940.

The Parade is still a main thoroughfare into the town centre.

Early fortifications at Le Braye Slip, St Ouen's Bay in July 1941

La Rocco Tower was hit during target practice by the Germans and badly damaged. It was repaired in the 1960s and returned to its former glory.

Funeral cortège for Oberleutnant Zepernick in November 1943 setting off from the Weighbridge area and heading for the German Military Cemetery at St Brelade's Church.

Now Liberation Square with the Jersey Tourism buildings. This area is popular with locals and visitors of all nationalities. It offers an ideal place for relaxation and reflection during the summer months.

Acknowledgments:

The publishers would like to thank the following
for their assistance in the production of this book.

Adler Archive
Franz Zurhorst
Joe Mière
Michael Ginns M.B.E.

This is the first in an occasional series of 'Then & Now' books. The next volume will be
"As Time Goes By - The Sixties." If you have any interesting photographs of Jersey in the 1960s -
whether it's you wearing a kipper tie, driving your Ford Anglia in front of a *__recognisable backgrou__*
or any other iconic picture of that time we would be delighted to hear from you.
Please contact Channel Island Publishing, Unit 3b,
Barette Commercial Centre, St John, Jersey, JE3 4DS. Tel. 01534 860806